FOREVER

BY
DAEL ORLANDERSMITH

★

★

DRAMATISTS
PLAY SERVICE
INC.

FOREVER
Copyright © 2015, Dael Orlandersmith

All Rights Reserved

SPECIAL NOTE

SPECIAL NOTE ON SONGS AND RECORDINGS

ACKNOWLEDGMENTS

Drunell Levinson
Okey Nestor
Heidi and Tom Sutton
Maude Campbell
Cassandra Campbell
Anna Steegmann
Kate Kubert Puls
Janko Puls
Jay Wahl
Jr Schaap
Elena Alexander
Neel Keller
Michael Ritchie
Jim Nicola
Eric Ting
Joy Meads
Pier Carlo Talenti
Adam Phalen
Mary Louise Geiger
Takeshi Kata
Hedgebrook Foundation
Kimmel Center for the Arts
Atlantic Center for the Arts

and to the countless people I've come across who've helped
in so many ways

Victor Cobos for telling me every night before going onstage
"TELL IT GIRL!"

and to my ancestors both familial and artistic, I stand on your
shoulders …

and
most importantly to the memory of my mother

Beula C Smith Brown — I hope wherever you are / you're smiling

FOREVER was originally commissioned and produced by Center Theatre Group at the Kirk Douglas Theatre (Michael Ritchie, Artistic Director), in Los Angeles, CA, opening on October 12, 2014. It was directed by Neel Keller; the set design was by Takeshi Kata; the costume design was by Kaye Voyce; the lighting design was by Mary Louise Geiger; the sound design was by Adam Phalen; and the stage manager was Young Ji. It was performed by Dael Orlandersmith.

FOREVER was subsequently produced by Long Wharf Theatre (Gordon Edelstein, Artistic Director; Joshua Borenstein, Managing Director), on January 2, 2015. It was directed by Neel Keller; the set design was by Takeshi Kata; the costume design was by Kaye Voyce; the lighting design was by Mary Louise Geiger; the sound design was by Adam Phalen; the dramaturg was Joy Meads; and the production stage manager was Lloyd Davis, Jr. It was performed by Dael Orlandersmith.

FOREVER was first produced in New York City by New York Theater Workshop (Jim Nicola, Artistic Director; Jeremy Blocker, Managing Director), opening on May 4, 2015. It was directed by Neel Keller; the set design was by Takeshi Kata; the costume design was by Kaye Voyce; the lighting design was by Mary Louise Geiger; the sound design was by Adam Phalen; and the stage manager was Sunneva Stapleton. It was performed by Dael Orlandersmith.

FOREVER

Lights come up. Character enters. Perhaps arranges photos on a table. There could be strains of Marianne Faithfull's "Ghost Dance" playing in background. *

Welcome
I am glad you're here / time to summon ghosts / time to give some voice / to make some sense / time to take a ride / let's take a ride
(Lights candle. Maybe puts on record here. Crosses downstage.)

As a child I dreamt
I dreamt of a city
A city of light
I'm Here
I got myself — Here
Paris
I am here in Père Lachaise / first time in Père Lachaise Cemetery
Paying homage to great people
And
Those people are Here but no longer here / BUT they are Here
(She points.)
In that direction there is Balzac and *(Points in another direction.)* Modigliani is there *(Points in another direction.)* and if you keep walking you will come across Piaf
Piaf
(Beat.)
I am in this place where greatness lives / rests / but still lives
I am seeking these people / these living resting people
These people who are really my family / who I really WANT to be my family
I'm thinking of Carol Cutrere in *Orpheus Descending* saying to Val

---

* See Special Note on Songs and Recordings on copyright page.

Xavier while in the graveyard, "Do you hear the dead people talking"
and then Val says "Dead people don't talk" and Carol says "of course
they do / they whisper LIVE LIVE"
(Slight pause.)
She's right — they do talk
And
There IS a movement within this silence / there ARE voices / whis-
pers both real and imagined.
I came to hear Colette tell me "you're a writer / where's your pen?"
I came to hear Yves Montand sing to me and blow me a kiss and I
see Simone Signoret giving him a playful slap and Apollinaire looks
on, laughing
I want all of them to look at me and smile and say "FAMILY"
And the people I pass on my way to see Oscar Wilde — we smile
at each other / point each other to directions that lead to Chopin /
Colette / Proust
All of us have come / ALL of us who are SEEKING / have come to
be with THESE people here in Père Lachaise — who beyond our
parents helped us give birth to ourselves.

I notice a girl.
walking in my direction
 — this young girl / more like a woman still with the presence of a girl
/ mixed race / not sure what races / she smiles at me / awkward — she's
awkward — she's dressed the way I was dressed at her age / this girl
— young woman — tries to dress strikingly / tries to look fashionably
unfashionable but because of her size / — because the clothing is not
made in her size OR if it is / she can't afford it, she tries to do a poor
man's mix-matched version of what she'd like it to be
And
Like me she can't quite pull it off
And
She's holding a book
And
The way she holds the book — the precious way she holds the
book —

I KNOW she reads a lot
I don't know her but I can TELL she reads A LOT
Like me does she find solace in books / music?

(Beat.)

I watch her walk
Her shoulders are hunched / TIGHT
Look at her
My god how I see ME in her hunched walk
And
I wonder if her mother like my mother (especially when my mother
was drunk which was very Often) possibly told this girl stories about
how when she was young and how her *(Does this in mother's voice.)*
"dress matched her bag which matched her shoes / which matched
her nails" and possibly this girl's mother like my mother also said
(Does this in mother's voice.) "I want you to look good because you're
a reflection of ME / you HAVE to be a reflection of ME"

(Beat.)
She looks at me
/ she looks at me like she knows me /

She looks at me like she REALLY knows me
Her eyes are present but also faraway.
Looking into her eyes / there is something otherworldly in them

She keeps looking at me
Fixed / drifting eyes
I can't figure it out — the look
Her look
I look away / I look back
And
Still she's looking
The gaze direct
Soft and direct at the same time
But
There is ANOTHER part that is too direct
There is softness and something overpowering

And
I'm getting angry
Real angry
(Pause.)

I turn my back and walk away.
I walk to Division 6 / grave number 30.
Jim Morrison
On Morrison's grave there are liquor bottles / scraps of paper saying
things like LONG LIVE THE LIZARD KING / THE LIZARD
KING REIGNS.
There is a small fence around it so no one can get too close
Morrison's headstone was stolen some years ago
So after that / there's been heavy security around his grave
There is a security guard who scans the crowd and as she looks at
the crowd / she can't quite understand what the fascination is
She looks at us and at certain points frowns / laughs / shakes her head
I'm looking at the corners of her mouth and there is a something
sarcastic / bitter in those corners
I think how if I had her job / I wouldn't just see myself as a security guard
As someone Anxious to BUST somebody
If I worked here / I'd see myself as a link / guide between the living
and the dead
I'd see these people who have come to see Jim Morrison and know
that they were SEEKING

I'd WANT to point my finger in whatever direction that person /
those people needed to go and say without saying "yes there was/IS
someone who felt/feels the way you felt/feel / they did it through
language / paint / song."
I would not stand there like this woman — sneering / indifferent
(Pause.)
Look at her — cynical as hell — out and out NASTY — God forgive
me I'd like to knock the shit out of this broad
(Beat.)
It is rainy in Paris today and not too many people are here but more
than what one would think.
Myself and few others are standing by the grave site
A woman — older — of Morrison's Generation throws flowers on
to his grave
A boy — young man stands by the grave site / headphones on
I look at him
He looks back
We nod
We connect

He's listening to the DOORS
I can't hear what song he's listening to from where I am / he's standing
on one side of the grave and I on the other but he is listening to the
Doors and he's moving his head / his eyes open and close
And
Whatever riff/word he's listening to RIGHT now
However/whatever is reaching him
Massaging him
Making him cry — because within a moment his eyes filled with tears
However
Morrison
Krieger
Manzarek
And
Densmore are moving him

Watching him — I too become moved
And
Watching him / I think of the very first time I heard "Light My Fire"
(Beat.)
I remember listening to WABC-AM — Cousin Brucie and sweeping
the living room floor.
Sweeping the living room floor in the house I shared with her —
my mother
This vermin-filled house with dead colored linoleum, booze stains
and cigarette holes
It's Saturday and I'm cleaning this living room floor / readying this
worn living room floor for my mother and her friends and their
weekly Saturday night drunk
Bottles of Johnnie Walker Red / white label bottles
soon to be emptied are waiting on the table.
I clean this floor — HATING what the night will bring
(Beat.)
Then Cousin Brucie announces *(Does him.)* "Cousins — Here's
'Light My Fire' by the Doors — we all know José Feliciano covered
it recently but of course COUSINS — the DOORS did it first and
I wanna play the uncut version for you — ALL MY COUSINS"

The Doors … hearing THIS — THIS "LIGHT MY FIRE" …
(Slight pause.)

I stop sweeping
The thing that plugged me in beyond Morrison's voice / Krieger's
guitar and Densmore's drums is Manzarek's organ solo
There was something otherworldly about that sound
And
I knew there was something BEYOND this broken down house
and being here with HER — my mother
Listening to that solo / I knew there was something BEYOND
But
I didn't know what IT was
(Beat.)
I keep cleaning
I had to keep cleaning 'cause if I stopped / I didn't know what I'd do
(Beat.)
So
yeah
The very FIRST ALBUM I buy is the Doors' first album

And
As I walked through the streets of Harlem carrying this Album / I
was met with many Stares
A guy on 125 Street says *(Does him.)* "Listenin to that white shit /
I should beat your ass"
(Becomes self.) And
I say *(As if to him.)* "yeah come on motherfucker!"
(Back to audience.) He keeps cursing
I keep cursing
I was eleven
And
The man that yelled at me was in his twenties
And
Although I didn't let him or anyone see it / I was frightened of him
I was FRIGHTENED of everyone/thing
But
You save face
You play hard

I continue to walk through the "make me wanna holler" streets of
Harlem carrying this album
And

I play it to death and listening to the Doors / led me to the Who /
the Stones / the Yardbirds / Steppenwolf and Arthur Lee and Jimi
Hendrix
And Jimi Hendrix led me to
— Howlin' Wolf
Muddy Waters
Mississippi John Hurt
Bessie Smith
Blind Lemon Jefferson
And
Reading the poetry of Jim Morrison *(As if to him.)* reading YOUR
WORDS Jim led me to William Blake / Comté de Lautreamont /
Rimbaud
(Beat.)
I brought lunch — a chicken baguette / cheese / fruit and a small
bottle of red wine (Bordeaux/screw-top) and a small glass
I want to eat and drink with my ancestors
I ask a tall blonde man / British accent where Richard Wright is buried
and he
hands me a map
I take the map and thank him
He smiles at me
And
It's a flirtatious smile
I smile back
And he sees me
I can't believe he sees me

And
in my head I hear laughter, background laughter *(Laugh.)* and a
background voice "What are you doing there / there in Paris? / you
don't belong there."
And within the laughter / and in / beyond the laughter / I can see
eyes / I can see the background eyes and above the background eyes
there are thick penciled-in brows and the eyes / the eyes that look
at me are blinking very slowly / they are red / blurry eyes / red
blurry / inebriated eyes and I suddenly smell scotch.
The smell of the scotch is strong and I realize it's HER

Mother

And
My skin starts to itch
I feel out of place
I feel dirty

I'm back in Harlem
Back in that house with her / my mother
My mother is teaching me how to read and write and count. I sit at
the kitchen table where on one side (the left) there are numbers
which went from one hundred and on the right of the table there
is the alphabet.
My mother sits / close/tight to me / says *(Does her.)* "Write your
name."
I do that.
I do that easily.
The alphabet / words are beautiful to me even then.
She says *(Does her.)* "Okay you got that / you understand that / let's
get to the math.
(Becomes self.) Math is hard
Not the counting but division and multiplying is and as I sit this
day and many days not understanding it / she slaps my head/face
from side to side / she punches me on my arms / pulls my hair yelling
(Does her.) "LEARN THIS / YOU ARE GONNA LEARN THIS /
I'LL BEAT YOU TILL YOU'RE BLOODY AS A BULL" *(Becomes
a child.)* "Mommy stop hitting me — please / stop"
The man — the beautiful man in Père Lachaise — he looks / asks
(Does him.) "Something wrong?"
(Becomes self.) I answer him
I answer him quickly *(As if to him.)* "no nothing's wrong / thank you"
(Pause.)
I almost said "you're beautiful / you're great / IT'S me / not you —
ME"
I watch him walk away towards Sarah Bernhardt's grave
I watch him walk until he disappears
There is an ease to his walk
He seems to move through the world with a fluid ease
(Slight pause.)
I want that Fluidity
I want that ease
(Pause.)

I can't believe I STILL can feel her slap — she's been gone / DEAD /
over twenty years but I can still see/feel/hear her laughing.
From the bowels of her southern grave I hear her / whisper / laugh
"What are you doing there? / You're not wanted there / NO ONE
wants you."
I'm years away from you
Miles away from you
I'm here in Paris
I got myself to Paris
Why are YOU here?
(She walks to another part of the cemetery.)
I walked to Richard Wright's grave
It is number 848.
The black boy/man who questions / challenged and refused to
"keep his place"
There are a few flowers
A few notes
Not as much as Jim Morrison
But
The flowers and notes are lovely — one of the notes merely says
"THANK YOU"
But
That
Thank you sums it all up

(Looks down at the grave.)
Mr. Wright — God how I would have loved to have a cup of coffee
or glass of wine with you
Ah — actually I can

I would have loved to have you as a friend
I'm glad you're buried here.
You should be buried here.
(She takes wine out of her bag and glass/looks around.)
Quick toast to you before someone catches me
(She takes a drink of the wine/puts it back in her bag. Beat.)
I've seen many pictures of you — many
I see your EXTERIOR / glasses and a gentle stern face
You knew at a very young age how cruel the world can be
And

You found the beauty / strength in words to reveal yourself in the face of that cruelty
(Slight pause.)
Richard, you wrote "I would hurl words into this darkness and wait for an echo, and if an echo sounded, no matter how faintly, I would send other words to tell, to march, to fight, to create a sense of hunger for life that gnaws in us all."
I heard the words Richard.
Those words got me here
(Pause. Then to audience.)

Your words got me here
Made me want to Stay here

There are times I did not want to be here
But your words
Made me stay
Made me want to stay
Your words did get me here
(Pause.)

And
now I'm here
Here in Paris
having the dream / conversations I always wanted to have with the people here
wanting to be held
embraced by THEM
these people
the-closest-thing-to-god PEOPLE

Yes
Their bodies are mingled within the earth
But
I DO HEAR THEIR VOICES
Have ALWAYS HEARD THEIR VOICES
But
I also hear another voice
(Pause.)
HER voice — my mother's voice

Beula
My mother
Pulling me back / yanking me back
(Pause.)

October 29 1959
I was torn from blood/guts/water
Spanked into consciousness
Spanked into living
(Pause.)

Pain
There was always PAIN
My birth was difficult / painful on her / to her
And
The difficulty of my birth combined with my father's passing in
1963 added to that pain
The pain extended itself to the house where she and I lived till her
death
The house did not comfort her
My father left her the house
Yet
It did not comfort or soothe
I wanted to know WHY that was?
I wanted to know the SOURCE of this pain
I wanted to know where it ALL began
Whenever I'd ask her about her life / she'd become irritable *(Does
her.)* "Why do you keep asking all these questions / it was a long
time ago"
(Becomes self.) There was something she would not / could not tell
She was cut off / closed off
(Pause.)

Especially
when it came to love
(Pause.)
Loving ME
She would tell me — especially when drinking — that she loved me.
A ninety-proof scotch-filled chain-smoked kind of love
She also told me this when not drinking / when there were moments

of softness / reflection
But
There was a strain to this sober admission
Like she had to convince herself / needed to convince herself that
she did love me
There was a HARDNESS to her
(Pause.)
But
There was also a SOFTNESS
And
A need for that softness
(Beat.)
The softness came to her through books/music/poetry
(Beat.)
Sometimes when she held a book / I would watch her
A smile would cross her face
Sometimes she would laugh aloud
She was soft / reflective when she read aloud
And
In those moments / I saw a HINT of a young girl
She told me about her grammar school teacher and how this teacher
made them learn and recite the poems of Paul Laurence Dunbar —
specifically "Dreams"

(Recites.)
"What dreams we have
And how they fly
Like rosy clouds across the sky
Of wealth, of fame, of sure success,
Of love that comes to cheer and bless
And how they wither, how they fade
The waving wealth, the jilting jade
The fame that for a moment gleams
Then flies forever — Dreams — Ah dreams"
(Pause.)

Her head goes back
And her eyes close
And
I SEE the YOUNG GIRL

I see a girl in a wooden school room that QUESTIONED
One of the few with pressed hair / a clean dress and shiny shoes
who stood before that class in that small wooden room taking in
the stares of everyone watching her dance her lips around the words
of Dunbar
And
I bet they were in awe
They must have been
And
Years later my mother in our pee-yellow / mouse infested kitchen
which did have some sunlight sat at our stained kitchen table
Savoring every word / every moment
And
As she recited the poem
(Slight pause.)
In those moments / in the pee-yellow mouse infested kitchen in
Harlem — I was transfixed
And
She was transported
(Beat.)

It was MY mother who FIRST unconsciously introduced me to Art
This confused / full woman reached for
Bach
Puente
Rogers and Hart
Dickens
Dunbar
She LOVED movies and although loved music was not fond of
musicals — or so she said
I often wondered — because she loved to dance and said she was a
great dancer why she hated musicals
(As if to her.)
Did you look at Ginger Rogers and Alice Faye and Busby Berkeley's
girls and think you could do it better?
Did you sit in that darkened segregated theatre and say *(Does her.)*
"that should be ME up there
Look at how Fred Astaire stole from Bill Robinson and the Nicholas
Brothers
Jean Harlow can't move

They're NOT that great / I could cut them down
I could really shake them down
That dance floor is MINE
ALL MINE"
(*Becomes self.*) You said you did like "Stormy Weather"
You said you liked Lena Horne
I remember saying to you how pretty she was
You agreed quickly but did not elaborate
Were you jealous of Lena Horne
Is that what the scotch was for?
When drunk you were not an aging overweight woman with
thinning hair
You were the girl with the nineteen inch waist
Out-dancing Ginger and Fred
And
You were just as PRETTY if not PRETTIER than Lena Horne.
(*Beat.*)

There were certain friends she had that did NOT drink
These UNSCATHED present people would sometimes come and
visit and she would make coffee
And
They would talk / drink coffee
I don't even remember her smoking in front of these set of friends
She would hold to every word they said
Her Eyes were OPEN
CLEAR
ALIVE
They talked of traveling to places
And
Leaving Harlem and building a home somewhere and retiring there
And
When she heard about this — her face would light up
(*Beat.*)
One of these friends brought one of their friends to the house to visit
And
This friend of her friend said (*Does him.*) "Oh man / I'm building a
House in Paris /
I was there in WW2 and I tell ya / I never felt so good in a place / I
had some family say to me 'man you need to stay here in America.'

And
I said to them 'well, I found MORE family there / REAL FAMILY
there and I love it and Man you can't beat the art / the Louvre —
oh man.'"
(Becomes self.) And
My mother looked at this Man — this friend of a friend and / she
really looked at him in WONDER / AWE and
Said *(Does her.)* "Paris / oh my god / that's great"
(Becomes self.) And
Then
She looked at me
And smiled
I smiled back
And
She looked towards Mount Morris park and whispered *(Does her.)*
"If I had only gotten to Paris — ONE time / JUST ONCE"
(Pause/beat. To her.) Paris is a wonderful place. I think you would
like it. I know you would.
(Beat.)
I keep thinking of those moments — moments when she was soft /
yielding — gentle
In those moments I confided my secrets / confusions
(As if to her.)
"Mommy why am I different?
Why am I so much bigger than everyone else?"
And she'd hug me
And hug me some more
But Secrets/confusions/thoughts that I told her in the soft/uncon-
scious moments were thrown back in my face when she was angry
Cruel comments come out of the ether
(Does her.) "Wanna know why no one likes you
You REALLY wanna know why?
You're fat / hateful / disgusting"
(Becomes self.) Then she'd change HER face / contort it — her face
I'd scream/holler
She no longer looks human
I'm six or seven looking into her face and she laughs
She laughs
She laughs hard
And

She is no longer human
I look into her face screaming "MONSTER;
MOMMY MONSTER
MOMMY MONSTER"
(Becomes self/speaks to mother.) You lift your nightgown
You show me your Caesarean Scar
This scar is large and brown / black around the edges
The scar almost looks frayed but of course it's not frayed because it
was done / MADE BY ME
A long time ago
A scar I made a long time ago coming through you
I stare at it
Wondering how I could have been born from it
How I could have born from YOU
And
In that moment you HAD to get me
YOU had NO choice
YOU HAD to get me back
YOU had to get me back again and again
YOU had no choice but to slap / kick / yell / punch
If YOU couldn't get it out and on to me / It would have destroyed YOU
After the beatings / I held you
Sometimes after the beatings / you made me hold YOU as YOU
cried
You would break down
Break Down
And
head long into tears
You'd cry as if you were the one beaten
And
Then
I had to hold you
I'd HAVE to hold you till you fell asleep
My oldest memory of having to hold her was when I was five
I was aware of the weight of her body
Her heavy breasts on my chest
Her breaking into tears / HER wailing "I miss my Mom"
This wail — these tears would come out nowhere and she's begging
(Does her.) "PLEASE HOLD ME"
So

I had to hold her
(Beat/pause. Talks again to the audience.)

After my father died
She did not allow me to sleep in the other room
I'd sleep as close to the edge of the bed as I could
She'd punch or kick me if I tried to inch away from her
(Beat.)
She wanted me — SOMEONE — ANYONE near
She NEEDED me — SOMEONE — ANYONE near
She needed me — SOMEONE — ANYONE
And
There I was in the darkness
Daughter
Mother
Husband
Lover
(Beat.)

I did not like touch
I did not WANT skin touch
I did not want skin touch of any kind
from anyone
Skin touch was scotch / cigarette filled and rumbling loose fleshed
women like her and her men — the Saturday night men she chose
that looked me up and down / their snake tongues darting in and
out touching themselves when her back was turned or when she
was scotch drenched or both …
Skin touch
Dank
Evil dark
Dangerous
That's what skin touch is/was
(Pause.)

The Summer I was nine Me and a girl named Tommy ('cause she
was a Tomboy) became friends
This one and ONLY summer Tommy and I became close
I usually went to South Carolina to visit my aunt
But

This summer I did not go
Tommy brought me inside her house and the house was filthy
All the kids — girls and boys — slept in one room
And
In this room / there were a series of bunk beds
They were three sets of bunk beds
For six kids
Six kids by six different fathers

And
There was the smell of piss
The kids were running in and out of the house barefoot / ragged
They looked like characters out of the movie *Sounder*
If one were to photograph it / it would like like a photo by Dorothea
Lange
Nellie, Tommy's mother, yelled / slurred *(Does her.)* "You little bastards
come on out heah"
(Becomes self.) Tommy looked at me

She looked away
And
Then looked down
We were both nine years old
(Beat.)

On the weekends — especially Saturdays / I would sit on the Stoop

Nellie might already be drunk by the afternoon
She often got drunk in the day
And
Certain days / you could hear her yelling / laughing / crying a
block away
And
On those days / when people really laughed at Nellie / openly
mocked her / Tommy would come over and talk to me
We'd talk about how our mothers drank
I'd say *(As if to her.)* "I hate it when she gets drunk / I HATE IT and
/ then all these adults want you to get up and dance for them"
(Becomes self.) And

Tommy would say *(Does her.)* "Yeah — my mother does that too
and all these drunk people all around me too — I hate it too"

(Beat.)

One Saturday / Tommy and I are sitting on my stoop
We're looking at Mount Morris Park (now called Marcus Garvey
Park) and Tommy says
(Does her.) "You know I climb the rocks a lot and I found a apple
tree in the middle of the rocks / it's real real small but I tasted one
the apples and it was real sweet"
And
I say *(As if to her.)* "Man I wish I could see that tree"

And
Tommy says *(Does her.)* "Come on / let's go"
(Becomes self.) And
Tommy and I climb those rocks and at first I'm afraid
Again
I'm big
And
Again
Awkward in my bigness

But
Tommy says *(Does her.)* "You can climb the rocks I won't let you
fall / I promise"
(Becomes self.) And
She sticks out her hand
And
She leads me to that place in the rocks where something grows
And

There they are — those apples
And
Tommy and I taste them
They're minute but sweet

In the middle of broken liquor bottles / used needles / torn scumbags
and more waste upon waste — they grew there — they were THERE

And
That day / The rocks we stood on were no longer rocks / they became
Mountains
And
When we looked towards the east

the Taino projects were not projects — they were majestic towers
And
When we faced west / the tenements were NOT tenements — they
were palaces
And
Below in the park / somebody had a radio on and we heard the
Young Rascals doing "It's a Beautiful Morning" … and even though
the sun was close to setting / that song in that moment
Was perfect and it fit
And
In that moment despite the fact that people shot dope in that park
and people got killed / got raped in that park —
In that moment / NOTHING would happen to us
Nothing Bad could happen to us
We stood on those rocks that became mountains where despite the
squalor — something GREW
How could anything happen to us
We were invincible
We looked at each other
We were friends
Nothing bad could happen to us
(Slight pause.)

Tommy held me by my hand
And
Helped me climb a mountain
There was nothing I couldn't do
(Beat.)

Finally we do climb down
We go back to my stoop
My mother is standing on the stoop and as I cross the street / she
begins to yell *(Does her.)* "WHERE HAVE YOU BEEN?"
And

As I get close to her / I can smell her scotch and cigarettes
And
I say *(As if to her.)* "me and Tommy were on the rocks"
And
I say — rather try to say *(As if to her.)* "I wanna go to Tommy's house."
And
Before I can get that out / She slaps me and yells *(Does her.)* "GET IN THE HOUSE NOW"
(Beat.)

She grabs my arm
Pulls me to her
Holding my arm as she stares at Tommy
Tommy is now her rival
My mother says to Tommy *(Does her.)* "It's best that you two don't play anymore / don't come here anymore"

Tommy stays in the vestibule and she overhears my mother say to me *(Does her.)* "That girl's mother Nellie is garbage and you see how ugly and dirty and raggedy she is / you don't need to be around her"
(Becomes self.) That night the grownups come
They drink
My mother drinks herself into her regular weekend stupor
And
As Usual / She demands that I dance for the adults to show them "the dances the kids are doing now"

I refuse

I make a point of being as nasty as possible
I make a point of making her look bad in front of her friends
I KNOW I will get a whipping for this

I don't care
It's not a whipping I haven't gotten before

She shoots me a look to let me know I'm embarrassing her
That night after her friends leave / I am beaten
I'm terrified but I've learned to save face

And
Play hard
I feel tears coming
But
I push them down
I push them way down — the tears

And
I say *(As if to her.)* "HIT HARDER"
She looks at me in disbelief
I NEVER said that before
That night I did not hold her
I did not hold her till she fell asleep
After that night / I never slept with her again.

(Beat.)
My mother's words caused a permanent split between Tommy and me
I'd see her randomly on the block through the years
And
She'd either look me up and down
Or

Turn her back
Years later / I saw her on the subway
She had moved away from her mother / from the block
She did not SUCCUMB
She made it
(Beat.)
She came over and sat down next to me on the subway
She was well-dressed and had on plenty of makeup
Our relationship and the shift — wasn't spoken about
At points / I look her directly in the eyes
She looks back at me
Then
Away
She got to her stop and said goodbye
I wanted to thank her for helping me LIVE
LIVE in MY BODY — if only for a day
But
I didn't have the courage to do so

(Beat.)
I also wanted to ask her as she was becoming herself / giving birth to
herself — purging herself of her mother and the ghetto we were both
born in / did she remember the viciousness of MY mother's words and
how did those words land? Did she use the words as ammunition?
And
Even now, forty some-odd years later / I wonder if she hears them
STILL
(Beat.)
Like I STILL hear her / see her / smell her / hear her
My skin / your skin still entangled
(Beat.)
There was this night / this one night that changed the scope /
changed the order of
things
Forever
(Beat.)
I was fourteen
And
It was Saturday

But

Not just a regular Saturday
This Saturday / I ask my mother if I can watch a film on her television
because her tv is bigger and she scoffed *(Does her.)* "Why can't you
watch it on YOUR tv?" And I say *(As if to her.)* "I need to see ALL
the images / can't see it on my tv — screen is too small"
Then
She frowns *(Does her.)* "What movie is this?"
And
I said *"Long Day's Journey into Night"*
Again
She sneers / scoffs
But she DOES let me watch it
Then
She says *(Does her.)* "Jason Robards and Ralph Richardson were so
good in this"
(Beat.)

In *Long Day's Journey into Night*, Edmund says: "Everything looked
and sounded unreal. Nothing was what it is. That's what I wanted
— to be alone with myself in another world where truth is untrue
and life can hide from itself."

Here was this man — this Irish man — who wrote about this family
— this late 19th Century/early Twentieth Century family — filled
with addicts and drunks
And
I sat there on the floor in semi-darkness — in her — my mother's —
bedroom watching / connecting to EVERYTHING — to HIM —
Eugene O'Neill

A Black Girl from Harlem living / seeing the same thing this
Irishman did
(Beat.)
Later that night in my room I listen to a blues compilation album
with Blind Lemon Jefferson on it
I listen to him over and over
And
Then
I go to bed
(Beat.)
I wake up
I look over at the clock and it says one-thirty A.M.
I smell smoke
I smell cigarette smoke
A man is sitting on my bed and says *(Does his voice.)* "don't look at
me / if you look at me I'll kill you / do you understand?"
(Becomes self.) I'm lying on my stomach
I bury my face in my hands

I don't answer
Again
He says *(Does him.)* "do you hear me?"
I answer "Yes"
He reaches over
He touches my ass
I'm wearing pajamas
He tugs at my buttocks through the pajamas

I go numb
I go cold and numb
I have never been so numb / so cold
He tears off a piece of the sheet and blindfolds me
He gets on top of me and tugs at my breasts and begins to rotate
his hips
The smell of cigarettes / sweat and his personal smell hit my nostrils
He then gets up
Walks back and forth between the living room and my room
He stops
Says *(Does him.)* "You got all white boy shit on the wall / all this
white shit"
(Becomes self.) He paces again
Walking back and forth
Mumbling
He goes over to the dresser
I hear him touching my perfume bottles
He paces some more again
As he paces he mumbles
I hear him say *(Does him.)* "Goddamn God God goddamn"
(Becomes self.) He comes back to the bed
He pulls off my pajama bottom
As he does this he says *(Does him.)* "You don't yell / if you yell I'm
a kill you / you hear me"
(Becomes self.) Yeah I hear you
(Pause.)

He gets on top / there is something sharp on my neck
It feels like a knife
He enters me
He's quiet

He's breathing heavy
Then he rams in hard
He rams in me repeatedly
I cannot breathe
I can't breathe

He senses this
Or

Did I say it
Or
Did he sense it
He pulls my head up
But is not rough
He pulls my head up conscious of the fact that I needed to breathe
And
He bucks up and down
His dick in and out
And
I can't scream
And
I feel his cum
I feel it leave him / and shoot into me
Hot
Then
Clammy
He gets off of me
He lights a cigarette
He lays beside me
He strokes my hair
He keeps stroking my hair
(Pause.)

He gets on top of me again
Rams into me again
I bury my eyes into my fists

I clench my teeth

And
He mumbles *(Does this.)* "God/oh GOD"
And
I say — in my head I say "God where are you"
He rams in me — in and out — screaming "GOD/oh god"
In my head I scream for him too — "GOD WHERE ARE YOU"
Are we screaming for the same GOD?
What kind of GOD allows this?
WHY are you are letting this happen to ME?
What have I done?

What have to I Done to YOU?
Where are YOU?
He slows down
He stops moving but is still inside me
His weight
His smell
He is still on top of me
His dick limp — still in my ass
Scum
Blood
Clammy
My eyes balled into my fists
Dark
Dark
It's dark
Or is it God
A dark God
No god
No more god
(Beat.)
He rolls off me
His breath is in my ear
He says *(Does him.)* "I wanna see you again / do you wanna see me?"
(Becomes self.) I don't answer him
I can't answer
I can't talk
I have no voice
My voice is taken

(Beat.)
I hear the hiss of urine near my bed
I hear him walk/run down the hall
I hear the door that leads to the street slam
I stay on the bed
I'm afraid to move

I make myself move
I have to make myself move — I pull off the blindfold
I roll off the bed
His urine in my face

Some it lands in my mouth
Some of it in my hair
I drag myself through his urine
I drag myself towards the door — her door
The pain in my ass —
Burning
Burning
I can't walk
Burning

I drag myself to her door
I make myself stand
I bang on the door screaming
She opens it
I run to her room
I show her
Turn around
I part my legs
She sees the cum
His cum
His cum in the crack of my ass
His cum stuck on my legs in spots
She cries
She breaks down and cries
I see myself in the mirror
One of my eyes is bloodshot
I take one of her perfume bottles
I throw the bottle at my reflection

Police arrive
They tell me not to wash
In the car they say it's a shame

They take me to Metropolitan Hospital
I think as I sit in the examining room how Billie Holiday died in
this hospital
I don't know why I thought that but I did / I thought "Billie Holiday
died here"
A West Indian intern comes in and yells at me *(Does this.)* "Hold
up your legs" as he gets me into stirrups

I want to slap him
Kick him
I'm too sore
I'm too afraid

MY legs are in stirrups
Silver cold instruments are inserted in me
The nurse is older and kind
I'm given pills to keep me from getting pregnant
I'm give more pills to keep me from getting venereal disease

I want to wash
I want to wash so bad
I want to be clean
I want to be clean
Clean
PURE
I'll never be pure again
The cops drive us back home
I take off the pajamas and throw them away
I put on a robe
I mix ammonia and bleach in the bucket
I know you're not supposed to do that but I do
I mop and mop the floor
The ammonia/bleach mix nearly causes me to faint
I keep mopping
I wait for it to dry
And
Mop some more
The floor dries
I wash the bucket and put it beside the bed
Like my mother when drunk / I keep throwing up — except I'm
not drunk
I lie on the bed but can't sleep
I lie on top of the bed with a blanket on top of me
I do not want to throw back the covers to get in the bed
Between the sheets is dark and big
I do not want to be INSIDE of anything
And
Even though I know he — the rapist is gone / he may come back

Come back and crawl in
I get up many times during the night to make sure the door is locked
In the other part of the apartment / I hear my mother crying wailing
I hear her bumping into furniture
I can smell her cigarettes burning
I can smell the scotch
The rape … *(Pause.)* MY rape — gives her an excuse to marathon drink

This is MY rape
MY fucking rape
She keeps reaching me / hugging me / the stench of her breath / the
flabby wetness of her skin reminds me of when I was forced to sleep
with her
And
SHE keeps crying / saying *(Does her.)* "He should have killed us
both / I wanna die / I WANNA DIE"
And

She just keeps
Reaching for me
She wants a Piece of me
I was his piece
The rapist
His piece
Now
I'm her piece
Piece of me
Piece of me
Leave me
Leave me
Leave me ALONE
(Beat.)
Later detectives come to the house
By now my mother is rip-roaring drunk and as she leads them to
my room / I watch them exchange looks
One goes to talk with her and the other sits on a chair near my bed
to talk to me
His name is Terrence O'Malley
He is broad shouldered and has a slight brogue
He is handsome with jet black hair and blue green eyes

As he asks me questions / he pats my hand
I throw up in the bucket
He grabs the towel on the bed and wipes my face saying *(Does him.)* "You poor poor girl / I am so sorry'"
(Becomes self.) He asks me more questions
His partner comes in and he gets up and they go off to the side and talk
My mother is on the phone and is moaning slurring on the phone about wanting to die
She comes into my room and looks at Terrence and says *(Does her.)* "HE SHOULD HAVE KILLED US BOTH"
(Becomes self.) Terrence looks at her and without his eyes ever leaving hers says
(Does him.) "NO he should have not killed you both / I'm glad he didn't and don't you think you've drunk enough / You're not paying much attention to your daughter / SHE got raped and SHE needs help / you may hurt but it didn't happen to you"
(Becomes self.) She stands there looking at him swaying back and forth and tries to say something but stops herself
She then starts to cry … again
And
She staggers to her room
Terrence looks at her and says *(Does this.)* "Jesus"
(Becomes self.) No one had ever stuck up for me before AGAINST HER
No one had ever come to my defense AGAINST HER
No one saw / wanted to see and he did
He and the other detective keep talking and I wonder what his house looks like
I wonder if he has any kids?
I wonder how old he is?
He doesn't seem too old
(Pause.)
I want him to take me to Ireland
I want to live with him there
If he's not too old / he could marry me
I look at him again
He is NOT too old
And
We could have a house by the ocean
Mrs. Terrence O'Malley

I want to be Mrs. Terrence O'Malley
(Beat.)
As the other Detective talked to him / I saw him looking at the posters on my wall
He looked at the poster of Thin Lizzy and looked back at me and smiled
He comes back over to me and sits down
He asks *(Does him.)* "You like Thin Lizzy?
(Becomes self.) And
I said "yeah they're great"
And
Terrence says *(Does him.)* "Phil Lynott — he's a Dublin boy like me"
And
I almost said "the next time they play / take me / YOU take me Terrence"
He hands me a card and says *(Does him.)* "if you need to talk / just call / again I don't know if we'll find this guy but we'll do our best / I promise"
I take his card and say "thank you"
For weeks I call myself Mrs. O'Malley
And
Phil Lynott is my big brother
And Eugene O'Neill is my grandfather
I think how one day I'm going to get to Ireland
How one day I WILL get there
And
When I get there / I hope Terrence O'Malley will be waiting for me
I never call him.
I never see him again.
I kept his card until I was twenty.
(Pause.)

Much later I remembered something Terrence said / he said *(Does him.)* "often people who rape / they know the person / not necessarily well / they might have seen you about the neighborhood / In your case / some of what you're telling me makes me think that"
(Becomes self.)
My Mother convinced herself that it was a man from the neighborhood who suddenly found God and became a preacher a week after my rape.

No one was ever arrested
And

The same way there was NO comfort for her in that house
There was now no comfort for me
(Beat.)

After the rape / after that
I feel a shift.
More than a shift / an alteration.
I feel an alteration in the way I see everyone/everything.
In the way I know/want/have to live.

(Beat.)
I needed to get out / I needed to get away
I needed to get out / get away
Even for a little while.
To get out / to get away from her — my mother
To get away from ALL of it.

There was THE VILLAGE

I went there as often as I could
Still lived at home but I walked those Village streets
East to west
West to east and back again
(Back.)
I hang in the clubs and on St. Mark's place heavily
In the clubs / I see
The Heartbreakers
The Ramones
Talking Heads
Television
Richard Hell and the Voidoids
Tuff Darts
The Shirts
Blondie
Mink Deville
The Bad Brains
(Beat.)

These years — fourteen becoming fifteen becoming sixteen — were
THE years
Books
Alternative music
Dreams of theatre
And
Studying theatre
Doing theatre
Doing theatre in the Village in a building on 7th Street called
University of the Streets
These years were the years of DISCOVERY
And
I saw there could be LIFE

There could be life without HER — my mother
(Beat.)
Around this time / I dress in black
Black
As mystery
Black as rebellion
Black not to fade away
But
To stand apart
The color black and guitar riffs
And
Drum solos
Black to meet the other kids
Outside kids
We — the outside kids in black
In CBGBs
In Max's Kansas City
We see each other on St. Mark's place
We nod/smile
We see each other
The rock n roll outside kids

I want them to be my family
I want to make them family
(Beat.)

She — my mother — tried to keep me with her / sometimes she'd say "be with me"
I'd look away
(Beat.)
She wanted to connect / desperately wanted to connect
One night I was watching Patti Smith on Tom Snyder on TV in my room
I keep watching her — Patti — talk / move
Patti was different
She was like a female Jim Morrison
I watch her and I'm mystified
I think "you can be a woman and do this
You can write / FEEL this way"
And
She — my mother — comes in and says "what is it about her you like / TELL ME / tell me about her."
I say "can you please let me watch this / just let me watch this / get away / leave me alone"
Her head goes down
She's hurt
I hurt her
I don't care
I just don't care

I needed to move / breathe
I needed to be away from her
I graduate high school at sixteen and a half
I double up on credits
I want to get out and I graduate in January '76
And
Later that year in late October / I turn seventeen
The following January / I'm in college
(Beat.)
A friend finds an apartment and wants me to move in
I tell her — my mother and she cries *(Does her.)* "NO — YOU CAN'T / YOU CAN'T LEAVE ME / I'LL KILL MYSELF IF YOU LEAVE / YOU THINK I'M JOKING? I'LL DO IT"

(Becomes self.) She sits on her bed
She grabs for me

She sits there on her bed eyebrow less (plucked to the point where
they no longer grow back)
Bloated and crying reaching for me
She reaches me / trying to hold me talking in her baby voice
She is not drunk as she does this
She is stone cold sober talking in her baby voice
I watch her
I watch her surprised
And
Repulsed
She cries out / "Don't leave me"
I look at her
I look her up and down
And
say
"you disgust me / ALWAYS disgusted me / I don't want to live with
FILTH like you"
(Beat.)
THIS statement / Being called FILTH … silences her
Silences us both
(Pause.)
She looks back at me stricken
We stare at each other
(Pause.)
I realize I do not have a love for her
And
she sees it
she see SOLID hatred that is and will always be there
I wanted to burn her
I wanted to kill her
I wanted to burn her down
Down to the ground
I would no longer be
Mother
Lover
Daughter
Husband

After that,
My interaction with her becomes short / intermittent

I walk away from her
Give her monosyllabic answers
Or
I don't answer her at all.
This period of time NOW comes to me as journal entries and snap-shots.

Snap shot — February 1989
She is now in her late sixties
But
Looks older
She's been diagnosed with diabetes since her forties
She is overweight
She buys an exercise suit and a pair of sneakers
(Beat.)
I look at the suit and sneakers and point and laugh
She takes in my laughter
She makes no further attempt to join the gym
She makes no further attempt of anything physical
After MY laughter
(Beat.)

Snapshot — March 1989
She sits on her bed in her semi-dark room sometimes with the television on / sometimes off
Her sister / my aunt had died
She went south to the funeral
On this trip / she tells relatives how I mistreat her
When she comes back / There is a deep sadness to her
When I go out and come back and she is often in the same place/ position I saw her in when I left
My aunt — her sister was her last and only love
(Beat.)

Snapshot — April 1989
Her eyes, cloudy / defeated
Her sight begins to go
A guy on the block tells me *(Does him.)* "Your Mom okay? … I walked her home cuz she said she couldn't see"
(Beat.)

Looking into her eyes / there is something otherworldly in them
(Beat.)

Snapshot — May 9 1989
She's admitted to the hospital
When I go to visit her / there is silence or hostility
Or
Hostility in the silence
I choose silence
The nurses become surrogate daughters and find her funny/delightful
When I go to visit / the nurses always stop to say *(Does voice.)* "Your
mother is one of the funniest people on the planet"
(Becomes self.)
One of the nurses / a pretty black girl about twenty-four says *(Does
her.)* "I told your mother about my boyfriend who cheated on me
but I also told her that I still loved him and know what she said?? She
said 'let him go / don't settle for less / you're more than that and for
him to cheat on YOU? … he's STUPID / I bet he failed everything
in school — old worthless ass / check his IQ — I KNOW he's
stupid!' … Your mother is so GREAT! / I LOVE your mother"
(Becomes self.) I think If she weren't my mother and I met her the
way this girl did / I'd like / LOVE her too
I'd find her funny / charming
And
I too would tell her my young girl/woman secrets
And
I too would delight her in maternal-like answers
(Beat.)
One day after the questioning about the house and more insults /
this time in front of one of the nurses — her surrogate daughters —
she says to the nurse/surrogate daughter *(Does her.)* "YOU are so
pretty / plus YOU work hard / too bad SHE" *(Becomes self.)* and
she points at me *(Becomes her.)* "doesn't do that"
(Becomes self.) And
The nurse / surrogate daughter looks at me / gives a nervous smile
and leaves
And
I look at her lying there in that bed
I look at her in love with sickness
She's in love with HER SICKNESS

And
I give it to her
And
I give it to her to full tilt
(As if to her.) "look I'm not the daughter you want and you are DEFINITELY not the mother I want / when you get out of here / I'm leaving / whatever money you have / if you feel like leaving to YOUR DAUGHTERS here in the hospital or to your nieces and nephews — go ahead / as for the house / a LOT of MY money has gone towards it / if you try and leave that house to anyone / I'll fight you or whoever / after you get out of here / I'm done with you / Forever"

I turn to leave and say *(As if to her.)* "I can't make it tomorrow / I'm working late"
(Pause/beat.)

I get back home
I get a phone call
A close friend of hers who was like a sister calls and says *(Does her.)* "I have something to tell you / it's not good"

(Becomes self.) My mother dies at seven-thirty P.M. May 18, 1989.
I left the hospital at seven
I was the last person to see her alive
(Beat.)
I call a cousin who lives nearby and he moans *(Does him.)* "God damn"
My mother's friend picks me up and takes me to Mother Cabrini hospital
We get to the hospital
The surrogate daughters/nurses are crying
And
They look at me muttering *(Does a voice.)* "I'm sorry / I am so sorry"
(Becomes self.) I'm handed her belongings
Clothing
Toiletries
And
I'm handed the last book she was reading which was John Steinbeck
— specifically *East of Eden*

I'm told I can go to the morgue to see her
I go down alone
The ride on the elevator seems long
It is not long but seems long
I get out of the elevator
I walk down a dimly lit hall / the walls are dull / off-white — gray really
The walls have streaks of dirt on them
I wonder why that is
Then I think the streaks — are they the last marks of the dead?
Are the dead leaving their marks?
The marks of people here — many no one knows about / cares about / have forgotten about
The junkies
Whores
Homeless
The elderly?
The ones without family?
The forgotten ones?
Is this the way they leave their marks as if to say "I was once HERE?"
I continue to *(Says in the spirit of the Doors song "The End.")*
"walk on down the hall"
I'm aware of the coolness/coldness of temperature
It was hot upstairs
Down here
It is cool/cold
The security guard greets me / mumbles "sorry about your Mom passing" as we walk through a cold room
I say *(As if to him.)* "that's alright / Don't you get scared being down here with all these dead bodies"
He smiles / says "No the dead can't do nothin' to you / it's the living you gotta watch out for"
He leads me through a series of even colder rooms
We finally get to her
The guard takes off the sheet covering her
And

Leaves me alone with her
She's wearing a brown house dress I recognize

She also wore this dress as a nightgown
I touch her
Her skin is alternately warm and cold but the coldness is really
beginning to set in
I stare at her face
I touch her face
Her mouth is open and one eye is closed
I wonder if there is a part of you that can see me right now
Can you see me now?
Can you see my fear?
Can you see that I don't quite believe that you are dead?
Why was I born to someone like you?
Why did you reach for me?
Why did you stroke my face?
Why did you slap my face?
Why did you beat me?
Why did you lie?
Why did you have me?
You
You
BITCH

(Slight pause.)
The expression on her face is one of RELEASE and surprise
If there was any pain / the RELEASE — surpassed the pain
(Beat. Talks to him.)
Richard Wright
(Slight pause.)
Richard Wright you said "If a man confessed anything on his death-
bed, it was the truth; for no man could stare death in the face and lie"
Maybe then THAT was the release?
She no longer had to LIE
To keep up the pretense of being things she thought she SHOULD BE
Wife
Mother
I think of the lies
I think of the burden of all the lies
How the lies made her reach for scotch
Sad / desperate / woman / sick / smart / confused
Little girl / woman

(Slight pause.)
Some say when one passes / that your entire life is shown to you like some sort of
panorama
(To mother.)
I wonder what you saw
Did you see yourself in South Carolina fields running in circles / reciting Dunbar
Did you see yourself sitting on midnight back porches dreaming of MORE
Did you see yourself taking dance floors with your nineteen-inch waist? And
Did you see me?
Did you question / see what you did to ME?
What we did to each other
(Back to audience.)
I keep looking at her
Her skin is beginning to darken slightly
In this moment I'd like to see the Caesarean Scar
I NOW want to see it
To see if I really came from it
From YOU
Go ahead and show me
Show me how I scarred you
Scarred you
Show me ALL your fucking scars
I wanna see you now
I wanna SMELL you now
I reach out and touch the scar
(Touches scar/whispers.)
This place
I come from this place
In / through you
I came from here
This hot / NOW cold place
I came from this NOW bloodless place
Of course
I have no recollection of being planted here
Or
Of CHOOSING to be a part of you

I wonder if I pushed hard to get out
To come here
To get out of YOU
Or did I fight to stay IN you because somehow I sensed the world
would be rough
I wonder if I tried to STAY
To STAY IN YOU / did I think I'd be safe
This place is now lifeless
And
This place will rot
But
I will not rot
I am here
I must make this place MEMORY
I MUST make you and this PLACE memory
(Removes hand.)
I make a point of locking my last image of her in my mind
(Beat.)
My last image of her in the cold room is not a snapshot
Or
fusion of snapshot/portrait
It is a pure portrait —
(Beat.)
I look away

I call out to the security guard who puts the sheet over her again
I walk back through the dim / cold halls
And
I go back upstairs into light and heat
The light/heat is disturbing
Voices and faces come at me
Worried faces/voices
(Does a series of voices.)
"Are you okay?"
"Can I get you anything?"
"Are you hungry?"
"Are you thirsty?"
(Pause.)
I don't want to be around all these faces and voices
I can't stand the light

I can't stand the heat
Nor do I want the cold/dark corridor of the dead
(Beat.)
I know she is dead
I saw her
She is dead
I believe it
I know it
I don't believe it
I don't know it
(Beat.)

After her death / I have a fear of staying in the house alone
I feel she will come back
Come back and show herself to me
Come back to GET me
To get me again and again
I sleep on a pull-out couch in the living room
When night falls / I lock her bedroom door
I feel as I lock the door / that I am locking HER in
The funeral takes place in South Carolina
The church is called Holy Rock
And
People swayed / sweated / wept
Pretended to weep / bringing attention to themselves doing their
Holy Roller dance
Saying "it was the holy ghost"
Others cried sincerely
My mother's cousins cried sincerely
They cried for her and for the young girls they ALL were in the South
And
How those young girls are no longer
They cried for her and THEMSELVES
They were close in age and knew they would be next
And
As I watched them cry / I realized some of them never had the
CHANCE to be girls
(Pause/beat.)
The casket is open
I watch people take her in

One of my uncle's kids takes pictures of her in the casket
I do not get up to see her
I've seen enough
This image in the casket is made up / perfected and stuffed
She is the way she would want to be seen
Lipsticked and perfected
I don't need to see her again
The real image of her / the real portrait was the one in the hospital
morgue
That is the image I choose to remember
(Beat.)
Everyone files outside
May heat in South Carolina is killer
(Beat.)
We all go to the back of the church where family is buried
(Beat.)
I look at them — this living family
These DNA people I'm a part of / But not
I look at them knowing I will never see them again
Never have to see them again
(Pause.)

The Casket is now in the ground

(Pause.)
She is gone

Officially she is gone

(Beat.)
Standing in the graveyard in back of the church / I see graves of
family that go back years
More than that
Centuries
I see the graves of ancestors
I just take it all in for a moment
These people my mother left
These people to whom she's returned
In bone
In ash

In dirt

(Beat.)

Back in new York
I go through her things
I'm anxious to know about her
and
I'm afraid to know about her
I come across many pictures
Some of them I've never seen
And
There are others I've totally forgotten about
In one of them she is in her mid-twenties
She is a vain woman / curious / made up like a movie star and posing
like one — totally aware of the camera
She is sitting on a lawn somewhere
The gaze towards the camera is ready
She wears a tight sweater à la Lana Turner
And
Her lipstick is perfectly applied
And there is an elegance
There is poise

(Beat.)
I find out she was a dancer
She was actually a professional dancer in a troupe
I ask my mother's cousin about her dancing days and she says *(Does
her.)* "Oh she was good / REAL good / EVERYONE's eyes were on
her when she was onstage"

(Becomes self.) I find out that man who raised me — my father was
NOT my biological father
There was talk of man who wore a raincoat in all kinds of weather
who ran women and numbers
There was talk of my mother being one of those women
There was talk of my having a sister
A child my mother had when she was a teenager
I ask one of my aunt's children — a first cousin about this and she says
(Does her.) "Look I was a child when that happened / IF it happened

/ I don't know / it was a long time ago / why do you want to stir this all up!"
She has home movies of my mother
I ask her for copies
She ignores my request
There are things — more and more things / unknown things / people unwilling to tell me things
There are things people simply don't know
There are things I'll never know.

(Beat.)
As a child I dreamt
I dreamt of flight
And
Now in this house
This house we lived in
You and I
I still dream
Sleeping/waking dreams
(Pause.)

I am standing in the bowels of South Carolina dirt / heat
Standing by your grave site
Which is next to your mother's
And
Her mother before her
And
Her mother before her
And
Slave ship songs I never heard of come to me
And
Visions of barefoot dusty southern girls telling stories on dark porches
Anxious to leave
Dying to try on urban high heels
You were one of those girls
But different
Poetry dangled on your lips
And
Your body swayed to all kinds of music
BUT

THEN
There was ME who scarred YOU
Scarred you
Unintentionally
I was sperm/seed
Planted / unplanned
Then
A Struggling water Womb baby
Whose entry was a specially made cut on YOU
On your abdomen
Where men leaned their heads
Where men stroked and kissed
And
Tongued their way to enter you
And
I by default
Unsmoothed that terrain
I made it jagged
Edgy
And
Dark
That jagged edgy/dark terrain
Where I was yanked from
Blood
Guts
And
Water
And
Spanked into consciousness
And
After that
You HATED ME
I undid your trick
And
You loathed yourself
I made it hard for you to turn the trick
And
You could never get ANYTHING right
I made it hard for you
To part your thighs and lips

To raise a penciled-in eyebrow
To whisper a whiskey lie
How hard was it for you
Tell me
Tell me how hard did I make it for you
My mother
My lover
My ghost riding whore
(Beat.)

Soon after her death / The house is taken by eminent domain
In her will / I'm left everything
Not a lot

But
Enough
Enough for a while

I take few things
"Enough-to carry-me-things" I call it
Many books/records
Few pictures
The photos are here with me tonight
Much of what was there — I leave / I don't want them near me
Can't have them near me
I move to an apartment in the Village.
I finally live around / with MY KIND /
(Beat.)
I take a trip to Paris
My First trip to Paris
As I walk Parisian streets / I feel beautiful
I want to be beautiful
I pick certain clothes
Certain make-up for different days
I change clothing/make-up many times throughout the day
I go to the Louvre
I go to Maxim's
I go dancing by myself at Hotel Costes
and
Ending up dancing with many people

Dancing
Dancing
In my skin
Feeling beautiful in my skin

I AM beautiful
I'm Here
I got myself — Here
Paris
(Beat.)

Today I dressed for Jim
I dressed up for Jim Morrison
And
Richard Wright
I wanted to be as beautiful / as gorgeous as I can for them
And
today / I read them my work
I read them some of my poems
And
Parts of plays written
And
Told them about poems I wanted to write
And
Plays I wanted to write
And
I heard them both say "YES"
And
The living/walking people around me understood
They walked past / smiled
And understood
(Pause.)
Jim Morrison, Richard Wright, Oscar Wilde. Chopin, Piaf, Proust
— are my family / I came to share my work with my family
My TRUE family
I spent the entire day
(Pause. Looks around.)
It's time to go.
Time to leave
Time to return this place to the dead

(Pause.)
I want to see Jim Morrison's grave again before I leave
I wonder if the girl with the book will be there
And
The boy/man with the headphones — is he still there?
And
That security guard / please don't let that security guard be there.
(Gets to the grave/looks around.)
Well the security guard is gone
And
The boy with headphones is gone.
(Looks around.)
The air is clean
And
a worker is toiling fresh earth for someone's return
Then
I see the girl.

(Beat.)
I see the girl on the other side of Jim's grave
And
She looks up at me / eyes again present / faraway but now teary
And
(Pause.)
This young girl now has the face of my mother
I feel cold/cool
Then strangely warm

MY MOTHER / looks at me
My mother's face tear stained but CLEAN
PURE
Tear stained
But
Smiling
And
She IS here
she is not tainted / or scotch filled
She is HERE
And
I see her

And
Her eyebrows are full
And
Her gaze is steady
And
She is PURE
She is here with ME
At Morrison's grave
And
The whiskey bottles — someone cleaned them away — all away
And
The sun's out now
and
It's quiet
Real quiet
and
She MADE it
SHE did make it to Paris
(Beat.)
I stand here by Jim's grave
Looking at you.
(Pause/beat.)
I think of you
And
the young girl you must have been
How that girl loved to dance
And
That young girl who had that baby — my sister and how that baby
was taken away?
I wonder what that day was like for you?
Did you fight to hold on to her — to hold on to my sister
and
I wonder did you think by having me / you'd forget and FINALLY
get IT right?
(Beat.)
I wonder if We any of us EVER get it right? …
Thank you
Thank you for The love of books
Writing
And

Paris
Thank you
(Pause.)
My mother is buried in South Carolina with her family /
(Pause.)
my family
But she's also in Paris
And
She's ALSO here
My whole family is here
bound by blood
By poetry
By music
By dreams
They are all here
Beula Camradora Lemmy Smith Brown is here with us
My mother is here
In my head/mind
My Mother in my head/mind
Here
She's HERE
Right HERE
She's here
Forever.
(Blow out candle. Lights fade. Music plays.)

End of Play

NOTES
(Use this space to make notes for your production)